MATERIAL WORLD

Wood

Wood

by Claire Llewellyn

W
FRANKLIN WATTS
LONDON•SYDNEY

This edition 2005
Franklin Watts
96 Leonard Street
London EC2A 4XD

Franklin Watts Australia
Level 17/207 Kent Street
Sydney NSW 2000

Text copyright © Claire Llewellyn 2001

ISBN 0 7496 6233 6

Dewey Classification Number: 674

A CIP catalogue record for this book
is available from the British Library

Series editor: Rosalind Beckman
Series designer: James Evans
Picture research: Sue Mennell
Photography: Steve Shott

Printed in China

Acknowledgements

Thanks are due to the following for kind permission to
reproduce photographs:

Bob Battersby/Eye Ubiquitous: 13cr; A.J.G.Bell/Eye Ubiquitous:
15br; Gary Braasch/Corbis: 26bl; I.Burgandinov/Art Directors &
Trip P.L: 21bl; Alain Compost/Still Pictures: 27cl; Daniel
Dancer/Still Pictures: 27tr; James Davis Travel Photography:
25cl; Bennett Dean/Eye Ubiquitous: 16br; Mark Edwards/Still
Pictures: 11bl; Gerard Fritz/Eye Ubiquitous: 8c; Pierre
Gleizes/Still Pictures: 21tr; S Grant/Art Directors & Trip P.L:
9cl, 17cl; John Heseltine/Corbis: 19cr; N. Holden/Eye
Ubiquitous: 17tr; Mike Jackson/Still Pictures: 10tr; Dani
Jeske/Still Pictures: 18b; Georges Lopez/Still Pictures: 19bl;
Darren Maybury/Eye Ubiquitous: 9tr; Tim Page/Eye
Ubiquitous: 10bl; Purves & Purves: 22bl, 22bc; H. Rogers/Art
Directors & Trip P.L: 14cl, 14bl, 14c; Phil Schermeister/Corbis:
20b; M.W.Smith/Eye Ubiquitous: 11tr; M.Shreeves/Eye
Ubiquitous: 13tr.

Thanks are also due to John Lewis for their help
with this book.

Contents

Words printed in **_bold italic_** are explained in the glossary.

What is wood?

Wood is a beautiful and useful material. It is used to make thousands of things. It is used indoors in homes, schools and other buildings, and outdoors in gardens and parks.

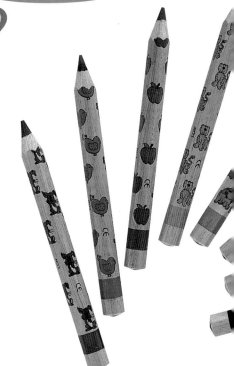

Looking at wood

There are hundreds of different kinds of wood. They can be difficult to tell apart. Each kind of wood is different from the others and is useful for different things.

All the things in these pictures are made of wood. Can you name them all?

Material words

Which of these words describe wood?

cold   thick   shiny

sticky   stretchy

heavy   stiff   solid

soft   strong

dull   hard   warm

hard-wearing

spongy   light

crisp   colourful

rough   smooth

thin

bendy   slimy

springy

runny   squashy

Take a look

Collect three items made from different kinds of wood. Examine them carefully. How are they different? How are they the same?

Wood is strong

Wood is a strong material. *Timber* can hold up the roof of a house, and sometimes the whole building! Wood stands up to a lot of wear. This makes it useful for furniture.

Holding up the roof

Wood is important in house-building. Big wooden beams are hammered together to make a strong framework that holds up the roof, ceilings and floors. Wood is also used to make door and window frames, as well as the doors themselves.

A wooden framework is strong but light. It supports the roof without putting too much weight on the house.

Holding up the house

For hundreds of years, wood has been used to stop houses sinking into soft, muddy ground. Some houses sit on stilts that raise them off the ground, out of reach of water below.

In places where there is danger of flooding, houses are built on wooden stilts.

Wooden furniture

Furniture is often made of wood. Wooden tables, chairs, beds, wardrobes and drawers are not only strong and hard-wearing; they also look good and are pleasant to use.

Fantastic fact

Wood is strong, but over many years it can be destroyed by the grubs of wood-eating insects such as the deathwatch beetle.

Wood floats in water

Most kinds of wood will float in water. That is why wood has been used to make all kinds of sailing boat - from small rafts to mighty warships.

Fishermen paint their boats to protect the wood from the water and bad weather.

A sampan is used for transporting people and goods.

Water transport

Boats are used on seas and rivers in almost every part of the world. They are a very important form of transport. Some are used to carry people and goods from place to place; others are used for fishing.

Modern boats

There was a time when all the world's ships - even the biggest warships - were made from planks of wood. This is no longer true. Today, large ships and sailing yachts are built of stronger, lighter materials such as plastic or steel.

A dhow is a wooden boat with a large sail.

A small dugout canoe is one of the simplest wooden boats.

Try this

Find a few wooden blocks of different kinds of wood. Put them in a bowl of water. Do they float or sink?
Do they sit high or low in the water?

Wood is a good insulator

Wood is a barrier to heat and sound. They cannot pass through it easily. Materials that stop heat and sound escaping are called *insulators*. Wood is a very good insulator.

barbecue fork

Wooden handles

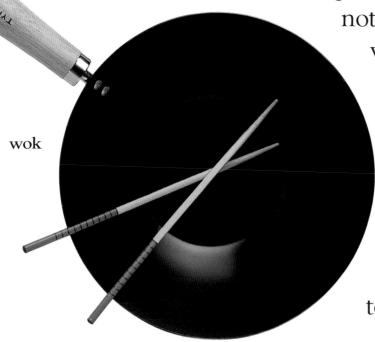

wok

Some materials, such as metal, allow heat to pass through them very easily; wood does not. That is why wood is often used for the handles on metal cooking tools and pans. The wood rarely gets too hot and is comfortable to hold.

Wooden walls

People who live in mountains and other cold parts of the world often have houses built of wood. The wooden walls trap the heat inside and keep the rooms cosy and snug.

A wooden mountain chalet keeps people warm even when the weather is cold.

Plucking the strings on a guitar makes a musical sound. The wooden sound box helps to make the sound louder.

Wooden instruments

Many musical instruments, such as the guitar, piano and violin, are made of wood. The sounds they make cannot escape through the wood. They roll around inside the instrument, making the music richer and louder.

Try this

Put two spoons – one made of metal, the other made of wood – into a mug of hot water. Leave them to stand for a few minutes. Now take them out and feel them. What do you notice about the spoons?

13

Wood looks good for many years

If it is looked after properly, wood can look good for hundreds of years. Every type of wood has its own colour and *grain*. Some are very beautiful.

walnut box

Compare the colour and grain of these different types of wood.

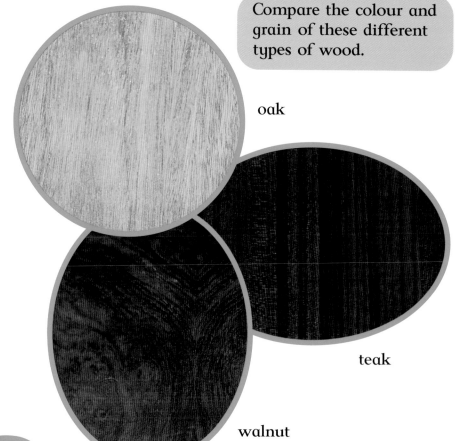

oak

teak

walnut

Colour and grain

Wood comes in different colours and shades - some are pinkish, some are golden; some are pale, some are dark. Each kind of wood has its own grain - a pattern of lines that forms in the tree as new wood grows each year.

Keeping water out

In the damp, wood does not rust like metal, but it will very slowly **decay**. A coat of paint or **varnish** helps to protect it. Wooden gates and fences have to survive in the open air. Brushing them with **creosote** helps to preserve them.

Keeping water in

All wood contains some water. It helps the wood to keep its shape. In warm, heated rooms, wood can dry out and begin to buckle and split. Polishing the wood with wax stops the wood drying out.

Polishing wood keeps it in good condition. It makes a smooth, shiny surface, too.

Take a look

Find a tree stump and look for the growth rings – the lines that form the grain. Now count the rings to find out how old the tree was. There is one ring for every year.

Wood burns easily

Wood is a material that burns very easily. This makes it a good *fuel* for cooking food and keeping people warm. But it also makes wood a fire risk. If a wooden house catches fire, it may quickly burn to the ground.

Making a fire

In many parts of the world, wood is the most important fuel. It can be collected easily and used to build a fire that gives out plenty of heat. Because wood is usually easy to find, it is a useful fuel for hunters and campers, and other people on the move.

In many countries people collect firewood to use for cooking and heating.

Making charcoal

Wood can be turned into **charcoal** - a black, brittle fuel that looks a little like coal. Charcoal is made by putting small logs of wood in a special oven so that they are slowly and only partly burned.

Charcoal is often used for barbecues because it burns slowly and gets very hot.

Wood catches fire very easily. In hot and dry weather, forest fires can sometimes burn out of control.

Fire! Fire!

Wood is a fire risk. In the past, when many more buildings were made of wood, town fires were a big problem. Shops, theatres and whole streets were often destroyed by fire.

Try this

Charcoal is often used for sketching. Try drawing with a stick of charcoal. Is it different from drawing with pencil?

Wood comes from trees

Wood is a **natural** material. It comes from the trunk and branches of trees. Wood can be sorted into two groups. They are called **softwood** and **hardwood**, and are useful for different things.

Under the bark

Beneath the bark a tree is made of wood. The wooden trunk and branches make a strong framework that supports the tree and helps the leaves to reach the light.

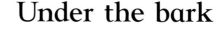

Fantastic fact

The world's biggest tree is the giant sequoia. Some are wide enough to drive a car through!

Soft or hard?

People who work with wood sort it into two groups: softwoods and hardwoods. 'Softwoods' come from quick-growing *evergreen* trees, such as pines and firs. 'Hardwoods' come from slow-growing trees, such as maples and oaks, that lose their leaves in winter. The names of the groups are not very useful: some softwoods are very hard and some hardwoods are soft!

Fir trees produce a softwood that is used for building.

Maple produces a hardwood that is used for floors and furniture.

From seed to tree

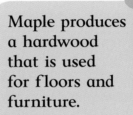

Trees are often grown in plantations. First, the seeds of the trees are planted in nurseries, where they sprout and begin to grow. A few years later the trees are big enough to be planted in a forest *plantation*.

A plantation of poplar trees. When trees are cut down, more are planted in their place.

From forest to sawmill

When trees are cut down, they are taken to the sawmill. Here the huge logs are cut into planks. They are piled up and left to dry. Then the wood is ready to use.

Cutting down the trees

When the trees are fully grown, they are ready to be cut down. The people who do this are called **lumberjacks**. They have powerful **chainsaws** that slice through the trees and send them crashing to the ground.

It takes just a few minutes for a lumberjack to cut through a tree with a powerful chainsaw.

Cutting the logs

The lumberjacks saw off the branches and cut the trees into logs. The logs are then transported to the nearest sawmill. Most are taken by truck or train. In some places the logs are pushed into rivers and allowed to float downstream.

Logs are taken to the sawmills on huge trucks.

Cutting into planks

At the mill, giant saws slice the logs into planks. This new wood contains a lot of water and needs to be left to dry. Drying out the wood makes it harder and stiffer, and helps it to keeps its shape. This is known as '*seasoning*' the wood.

At the sawmill, a large saw slices the logs into planks.

Try this

Find a thin piece of wood and soak it in water for two days. Then put it somewhere warm to dry. What happens to the wood as it dries?

Every part of the wood is used

Wood from the sawmill is used in many ways. The best timber is used for building, furniture and floors. The rest is used to make paper or wooden boards.

Using the best

The seasoned timber is taken to factories and timber yards. The best softwood is used for building. The hardwood is used for furniture and floors. The wood that is not so good is used to make wooden boards.

beechwood stool

cherrywood chair

Wooden boards

There are different kinds of wooden board. Plywood is made from thin layers of wood that are stuck together. Chipboard is made from small chips of wood and sawdust that are glued together. Sometimes a layer of hardwood is laid on top of the board to make it look like solid wood.

chipboard covered with a thin layer of hardwood

plywood

chipboard

Making paper

A lot of softwood is taken to paper mills. Here it is chopped up and mixed with water to make **wood pulp**. This is dried and flattened to make paper.

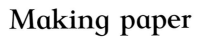

Wood is used to make paper, one of the world's most useful materials.

Try this

Make your own chipboard. Mix 2 tablespoons of sawdust with some wood glue until you have a sticky mixture. Put this into a matchbox. When it is dry, peel off the cardboard box.

Wood is easy to work with

People have worked with wood for thousands of years. It is an easy material to cut and shape. It is not only used by carpenters, but also by artists and craftspeople.

Working with wood

It takes skill to work with wood. For building and furniture-making, the wood is usually sawn along the grain and cut into carefully measured pieces. Carpenters use a wide range of tools such as saws, planes, hammers and screwdrivers. These all have metal blades.

Carpenters use many tools. Can you name any of these?

Joining wood

Two pieces of wood can be joined together with screws or glue. The finest wood-workers cut the wood into special shapes that fit together very tightly. These shapes are known as joints. Many of them were invented hundreds of years ago.

The dovetail joints on this drawer fit together like the pieces of a jigsaw. There is no need for nails or glue.

This wooden mask was carved by South American Indians.

Carving wood

Wood isn't just used to make useful things. It is often used in art and craft. All around the world, people have carved, and still carve, pieces of wood into pictures, statues and masks.

Try this

Find an old piece of wood and rub it with sandpaper. What happens as you rub away the surface of the wood?

25

Looking after forests

Around the world people are using more and more wood - for fuel, for building and for making paper. This means we are cutting down more trees. Trees that are cut down should always be replaced. Many should be left alone.

A crop of wood

In many parts of the world, trees are now being grown as a crop. As each tree is chopped down or 'harvested', a new one is planted in its place. This is the best way for us to use wood.

Fir seedlings in a plantation.

A land without trees

In other parts of the world, when trees are chopped down, nothing is put in their place. Without trees, the land begins to change. When it rains, the water pours down the hillsides, washing away the soil. This leaves 'dead' land where nothing can grow and where wildlife cannot survive.

Trees help to protect the soil. Where trees are cut down, the soil may be washed or blown away.

Orang-utans live in the tropical rainforest. People are trying to save the forest before these animals become extinct.

Destroying habitats

Every year millions of trees are cut down in *tropical* forests so that their timber can be sold. But the forests are home to animals and plants that cannot live elsewhere. These living things may become *extinct* if their *habitats* are destroyed.

Fantastic fact

Trees supply us with many useful things besides wood: rubber, cork, fruits, nuts, fats, gums and oils.

Glossary

Chainsaw   A powerful saw with an engine that is used to cut down trees.

Charcoal   A fuel that is made by baking wood.

Creosote   A dark, oily liquid that smells like tar and is used to protect wood.

Decay   To rot.

Extinct   No longer living on Earth. An animal becomes extinct when none of its kind is left alive.

Evergreen   Trees, such as pines and firs, that do not lose their leaves in winter.

Fuel   Wood, coal or some other material that can be burned for heat and power.

Grain   The pattern of lines in a piece of wood.

Habitat   A place where wild animals live because it provides them with food and shelter.

Hardwood   The name given to wood from trees that lose their leaves in winter.

Insulator	A material that prevents heat and sound from moving from one place to another.
Lumberjack	A person who cuts down trees in the forest.
Natural	Found in the world around us.
Plane	A carpenter's tool for smoothing wood.
Plantation	A large piece of land that is used to grow one type of plant such as softwood trees.
Season	To allow wood to dry out so that it is ready to use.
Softwood	The name given to wood from evergreen trees.
Timber	Wood that is used for building or carpentry.
Tropical	From the tropics: the warmest, wettest parts of the world.
Varnish	A clear liquid that protects the surface of wood.
Wood pulp	A mixture of wood chips and water, used for making paper.

Index